Memoir of a
Teenage Love Affair

Christopher Black

iUniverse, Inc.
New York   Bloomington

iUniverse books may be ordered through booksellers or by contacting:

iUniverse
1663 Liberty Drive
Bloomington, IN 47403
www.iuniverse.com
1-800-Authors (1-800-288-4677)

Because of the dynamic nature of the Internet, any Web addresses or
links contained in this book may have changed since publication and may
no longer be valid. The views expressed in this work are solely those of
the author and do not necessarily reflect the views of the publisher, and
the publisher hereby disclaims any responsibility for them.

ISBN: 978-1-4401-5459-1 (sc)
ISBN: 978-1-4401-5458-4 (ebook)

Printed in the United States of America

iUniverse rev. date: 07/20/2009

To Margo

Contents

Say your dreams, they all have changed.
Well, my smiles, they all have faded.
And the thoughts that used to seem so
pure in my heart,
they now feel jaded.
Because I want to feel like I did.
And I want to feel innocence.

— Darius Rucker

1

An Older, Wiser Man

The following entries I wrote from 2000 until 2002. They spanned my senior year of high school, until the summer before my junior year of college. The entries revolve around my daily life, my philosophies, and my general ramblings. The overarching constant, however, is my relationship with a girl named Maggie.

Maggie went to high school with me, and was a year older than me. In high school I wasn't very smooth with the ladies. I needed a date to my junior prom, and my friend set me up with Maggie. We had a great time at prom. When I dropped her off, she kissed me on the cheek. I was on top of the world. I had hoped to continue a relationship with her following prom, so I called her. She never called me back.

I ran into Maggie at a movie theatre a few months later. We became friends and kept in touch. I always wanted more. She was so different from other girls I knew. She was so passionate, intelligent, and I felt so comfortable around her.

When we would hang out, we had a great time, but nothing romantic ever happened. I was shy and scared, so I never made a move on her. We didn't talk for a few months and I almost forgot about her. I figured nothing would come of it. Then, my friend who had originally set us up on our prom date ran into her somewhere. He asked her why she and I never dated and she said it was because she didn't think I was interested in her because I never attempted to be romantic with her. This is where my entries begin.

Following my junior year of college, I didn't keep in contact with Maggie. I heard she got married to some guy and moved to Baltimore. Then, fate struck. I was in a store in my home town, and I saw her. She told me she was divorced, so I asked her out. It had been ten years and it was fate.

We dated for five months and then it ended. I called her one Friday night and she never returned my call. I know why. There were a plethora of reasons. I brought up several things to her during our second chance. I felt like we were married. I felt like she took me for granted. I'm twenty-seven years old and I want to know the relationship I'm in might lead to something more. We dated five months and we weren't technically boyfriend and girlfriend. A few days prior to her not calling me back I bottom lined her. I told her I wanted to get more serious. I wouldn't have minded some of the things I complained to her about, if I knew she was committed to me, and there was a light at the end of the tunnel. True to her nature though, she couldn't commit. I think she's scared and I will take that thought to my grave. So the following is an excerpt of an email I composed, but never sent to Maggie a few days after we stopped talking.

> *I feel like I just got divorced. Who's going to see Ryan? You see the first set, I see the second? Let me start off by saying you're awesome. I never met anyone like you and I never will. You introduced me to so many things. That's why I always liked you. You are so well rounded. So here it is. I'm going to send you my book, you're going to read it, and you're going to say, "how it is possible that someone loved me so much." Forget what I've written. Bottom line: You need to tap into your emotions. I'm here. I want*

to talk to you. I know you're going through a lot with being on your own, divorce, making it on your own. I know. I want you to open up. There's so much inside of you, but you block off. It's like if something doesn't agree with you, you cut it off. Well, you know what, you can't do that. I know you think I'm a clown, but I'm not. It's a self preservation mechanism. You don't show emotion. You're so stubborn. I want to take you in my arms and hold you, but you're non- responsive. It's like, there's something missing. And I was reading my journal from ten years ago, and it's the same old story. I get the feeling that you're dead inside. In high school, you used to be vibrant and full of life. I know I haven't changed your feeling, but either way, I think you need to get that back.

Less what you said and more what you did: On my birthday, you went night skiing and left me with your brother's wife. I know it was a skiing trip but I thought it was an "us" trip first. That hurt me. So I might have made some comments that you didn't like, but it goes both ways. I was just trying to be real with you, so if you can't be honest with the person you love, who can you be honest with? You totally think I'm a joke and you always have. I want you to be real with me, and that's all I've ever wanted. Who gives a shit if I like rap and you don't. We need to dig deeper than that. I love you. And I don't know how to show you. You get offended when I talk to you, but I want to have a dialogue.

2

Penncrest High School:
Spring Semester,
Senior Year

April 12, 2000

1

T'was a brisk, spring evening when I embarked upon a heroic journey. I lived in the large house on the hill and I was oblivious to the world. I was knowledge less, as I was seeing for the first time. What lay ahead of me, I knew not. Open and fearing, I set off on my life. My journey begins tonight.

Tonight I intend to get to the point, what is real. I want to understand myself and express what I'm feeling. Let me restate my goal in my life. I would like to finish college with a degree in psychology. I would then like to set off into the world. Travel the world, in search of answers to all of my questions. I would like to read and gain as much knowledge as I can during this time. I would also like to keep notes of my travels and document when a significant revelation or experience occurs in my life. When I feel the time is right, I will live on an island. There, I'll write about my life and ponder the meaning of life. If I do this, I will have truly lived, and only then, I will be satisfied.

What do I not want to do? I don't want to end up like most people I know. I don't want to finish school, get a decent job, making good money. I don't want to have a wife, kids, a big house, or family get togethers. If this happens, then my life will be a waste.

I must think. No one thinks in the world. I consider myself to be the most unique person in the world. I want to be true and real. This is why with my first writing; I would like to discuss my relationship with one, Maggie Pinski.

For two years now, we've been seeing each other as friends, at least I think. But that is what I mean. I have known a girl for two years, and I don't know where our relationship is. This is because I haven't been real with myself. When I'm around her, I constantly joke. The fact of the matter is I'm not the real me with her. She makes me feel great, and we have a great time, but she really doesn't know me. I don't think she could possibly fathom who I am. I assume she thinks I'm some average kid who just jokes a lot.

Well, tonight I have made a decision that I will ask her about how she sees our relationship. I then want to tell her, or try to explain, well, me. I've never done this before and I don't know how she'll react. I really like her and I want to get to know the real her. I hope all goes well.

April 18, 2000

2

Wow, some shit happened with Maggie. The other night she invited me down to Baltimore for two days and two nights. The first night before I left, I took advice from one of my co-workers, Major, at Friendly Mart. He told me not to put the moves on her. Don't do this because she'll be expecting me to. When I don't, she'll be pleased with me, and I'll get it back tenfold when we actually do make love. This sounds like good advice. Plus, I like Maggie more than a girlfriend, a good friend, or a lover. She's more than that to me. I didn't want to just have sex with her and be her friend. I want all of her and I want to give her all of me. I don't want to have a fake relationship. I want to have something that is real. I think Maggie might understand this.

The first night Maggie asked me where I wanted to sleep, and I told her I didn't care. Then she took out a sleeping bag and put it on the floor next to her bed. Finally, she took out a really fluffy air mattress she got for Christmas. She then said, "Well, I guess you can sleep in my bed if you want, but you have to sleep on that side." "Sure" I said. So, we're in bed for about two minutes with the lights off, and the music on soft and we haven't said anything. At this point, I haven't made a move on her, sticking to my plan. She then says, "So why did you come here?" Jokingly, I told her, "to get out of my house." I asked her why she invited me down. She wouldn't answer me and she rolled over. After another couple minutes she said, "This bed is too small." She got up and went in the other room. I'll tell you what. I wasn't going out like that. She's better than that, and I'm better than that. I need to tell her how I really feel, because the first time I told her, it didn't come out right. Then it will be alright. I just want something real.

3

The University of North Carolina at Charlotte: Spring Semester, Freshman Year

3

Well, I'm on this train back to school for about three more hours. It takes ridiculously long because to drive to Durham it only takes an hour and twenty minutes, but on a direct train it takes three hours; go figure.

Yeah, well, the last thirty seven hours have been a trip for me. A lot of shit has happened. I didn't go to sleep last night. It was my last night home before second semester. I was with Maggie, and it was amazing. I should start off by saying I did it. I told her everything I was thinking and feeling. I told her that I wanted to have a bond with her. We're always saying that nobody truly knows anybody. I told her I wanted to know her. I said I wanted to be more than a friend and more than a lover. I wanted our relationship to be unique and I didn't want to put a title on it like boyfriend or girlfriend. She understood and agreed.

I encountered a startling revelation last night that changes things. Maggie is a virgin. I found this hard to believe because she's had several boyfriends that went out with her for more than a year. She said her reason for not having sex is because she is afraid of screwing up her life. She doesn't believe in abortion, so if she did somehow get pregnant, she would have to keep the baby. That is the best reason I've ever heard. I mean, at least it isn't that she's waiting until marriage.

I care a great deal for Maggie. I've been seeing her for almost two years without sex; it is by no means the only thing I want. Her being a virgin, however, makes our relationship even that much more special. I can tell you right now, there is no other person in the world that I would lose my virginity to. I don't know. It just feels so right being with her; like it was always going to happen. Also, being that we're both virgins and we've waited this long, it would mean so much. Experiencing it for the first time, as nervous and as scared as we would be; would give us a bond like no other.

I feel so strongly about being with her for my first time. I would like to do it. She's told me her feelings about why she doesn't want to and I respect them. I can't force her to do anything. If we're going to do this, the feeling must be mutual. I can tell her this. It's okay to be afraid and scared. That's part of the experience. We'd have to use solid protection. I personally feel that if enough anti-pregnancy procedures are taken, the risk is low enough that I'd be willing to take my chances. I can't speak for her. She might just need more time. I don't know and she might not either. All I can offer her is my caring and support. I invited her down to my school before she's done her break. I need her to come down so I can show her my life down here. It would also be a perfect opportunity to discuss further the thought of making love or possibly actually doing, because I think I'm ready now.

January 18, 2000

4

This is probably going to be the shortest entry ever. Today at dinner I met some girl named Ariel. She's a cute, blonde haired girl. She lives on the third floor of my dorm. She seemed like she had an alright personality. If I got to know her better, she would be a definite candidate for girlfriend. Okay, that's all I wanted to say.

January 21, 2000

5

Wow, I probably shouldn't have written that last entry, but whatever. I have nothing terribly important to say, but I just felt like writing. Maybe I wanted to write about people trying to find their identity.

I really like Hootie and the Blowfish. I guess you could say they're my favorite band. The fact of the matter is that I know very little of their lyrics. In fact, I don't know much about them at all. Which leads me to a brilliant observation, in my life; I've never known that much about anything. I mean, I've never really taken something and made it completely part of my life, embracing it, and knowing everything there is to know about it. I mean, Hootie and the Blowfish is my favorite band, and I've never seen them live. I really like Darius Rucker's voice. I also like the beats in their songs. Finally, I usually like what they sing about. Their girl being drunk all of the time, racism, parents dying, love. They have some great upbeat songs like "Only wanna be with you," but they have good slow stuff like, "Goodbye," and "Gravity of the situation," remade, but still solid. They also have some soul in them, I like that. After their initial success, their popularity decreased. I always liked them; I guess it wasn't a band wagon thing.

I'm afraid, as people, we might cling onto things, to be a part of something. Like with Maggie; she's obsessed with Bob Dylan. The man was great, don't get me wrong, but to her, he's a god. She's been to like twenty six of his shows or something. I am so jealous. I want to be able to do that so much, but I can't. I don't see how anyone can get that involved. It's amazing to see her when you put her and Dylan together. I guess it all goes back to finding yourself. I guess, in a way, Bob Dylan has shown Maggie a part of herself. And I think that's awesome. She once said, "You analyze everything." I think you have to. I don't know; Hootie just does it for me. I want to find myself.

January 28, 2000

6

I actually want to go to bed soon, but I felt it very necessary to write this down tonight, so I never forget it. J-Will and I were talking tonight. I told him that just recently, like over the last three weeks, I've had an empty feeling inside of me. He told me that is the way his entire life has been. He has two things in his life, General Hospital and Carolina basketball. He said the thing that keeps him going is the hope and anticipation, that maybe; just maybe, something truly good will come into his life.

My deal is that ever since second semester started, I've had nothing to look forward to. I study and go to class all week, and on the weekends I just sit and watch television. That wasn't the true college experience I was looking for. I want to go to Charleston on April ninth to hear Hootie and the Blowfish.

I hope I get into American University. Even if the social life sucks, I can always go to the city. Since I'll have a car, I'll be able to see Maggie on weekends or something like that. Anyway, I won't have to stare at a TV all weekend. I can go out and experience life, like roaming around a fascinating city or go see someone I really care about.

February 14, 2000

7

I might have written about it before, but I want to answer a very basic question that everyone assumes to know the answer to. The question I will state in Khlil Gilbran fashion by saying… and what of love master?

Today is Valentine's Day, so I might as well bring it up tonight. I don't really believe in love. I don't think I've ever experienced it. What is love exactly? Here, let me get a book definition. Webster's states: Love: a strong liking for someone or something; a passionate affection for another person; the object for such affection.

Quite the contrary, I have loved many people in my day, and hence, love exists. But, is it required that one should know the whole person before one can be truly be in love with another? If this is the case, no one has truly been in love. The definition for love is rather broad, therefore, by its definition; many people may be in love. Its fault lies in the fact that it lacks a reference to time. Is it not true that you can like someone very strongly one moment, and then the next moment have a strong dislike for them? It is indeed possible.

For two years I have known Maggie Pinski, and because it's Valentine's Day, I feel like I'm entitled to talk about it. During the course of our relationship, I think

I've fallen in and out of love with her an infinite number of times. Sometimes I strongly like her and sometimes I strongly dislike her, or more, what she does to me.

When I think of Maggie, so many emotions come to mind. If love is as simple as its definition, I am in love with Maggie Pinski. I don't think it is, however. I want to know the "true" her before my final love/hate feelings for her are solidified.

Some of the people are Mom, Matt, Tony, Mike, Maggie, I mean, those people just get me. The only person I think gets me down here is J-Will, but even we have our differences. It feels so good to be around those people who understand you. I guess it is okay.

Hopefully I will hear if I got into American on Monday. If I do, that will be a big relief. I can just concentrate on my work without that hanging over my head. I think in the next two weeks I will make an attempt to open up to people, so maybe I can find my niche here socially before I leave. I think it will make me feel a whole lot better about my experience here.

March 26, 2000

8

A couple of eventful and interesting things happened today, on an otherwise uneventful, idle Saturday night/day. I guess the first one I'll ponder will be that I saw the movie Traffic. One of the subplots was that this girl got addicted to free basing coke. Then she graduated to shooting heroin. When she injected it into, her, I couldn't watch. I could hardly sit through that part of the movie. Normally I would blow it off and say it's no big deal, but for some reason I was thinking about Dave and it infuriated me. I guess I was disgusted and angry and frustrated because like my brother, she gave up all of her freedom to drug addiction. And I don't mean that this girl was at the top of her class and was the vice-president and I was angry she was ruining it. That doesn't mean much to me. I care that she willingly took her own freedom out of her hands and gave it to the drug. I mean, she was fucking the dealer just to get the stuff, she didn't care, and she was a slave to it. It made me sick just to watch it. Like she, as Dave, thought that's it. Thought there was nothing else out there. How weak and misguided could they have been? Because, like getting good grades, a lot of money, power doesn't bring you happiness, neither do drugs. You aren't truly happy with either of these things. In essence, money and power can be like a drug for some people.

The movie's point was pretty much that the war on drugs is pointless. It is a war that is fought on the home front, against our families. So you can combat the supply all you want, but the true problem lies in the demand for the drugs. The problem lies at home.

The other possible thing I could talk about is that my mom might be moving across the street from Maggie, which definitely would be interesting. It's not confirmed yet, so I'll have to wait and see. I will comment later on that.

March 27, 2000

9

For some reason, probably because its spring break and I'm bored, I feel like writing yet again. This time it's about me. In sociology, we learned about "Cooly's Looking Glass Self" perspective. This is when a person's self image is composed of what kinds of responses you get from people. From these comments, you internalize them, and they make up your self image.

Almost everybody down here doesn't get me. I mean, at home, there are a number of people who get me. I mean, they might not understand everything, or get the big picture, but they accept me, and understand why I do what I do.

March 29, 2000

10

Time is drifting. This rocket has got to roll. Ain't nothing like the Climax Blues Band. Tonight I saw the movie "Almost Famous." It was solid and about a half an hour ago I really wanted to write about it. Now I don't. I do want to write about several other things.

I finally got an e-mail from Maggie. Well, it's only because I invited her to a Bob Dylan show. I've accepted the fact that she is the type of person that doesn't call back. If you want something, you have to initiate the action. I guess I'm okay with that.

Later this month I'm going to buy a ticket to the Center City Fest. Bob Dylan, Hootie and the Blowfish, Indigo Girls and others are going to be there. Hell, it was only twenty-five bucks. I'm really excited about this. This will definitely be an experience. For me to say its highly anticipated would be an understatement.

I invited Maggie, but the fact remains, she probably can't go. It's all right. It's a long ways away. I would like to think I would do it for her, but, in reality, I probably wouldn't be able to make it. I'm okay with that. I thought of something else, because Maggie can't make it.

Okay, well, there are a couple of other kids here at school that are going, but I don't really enjoy their company, so I think it would be better to go alone. It's alright though. That might be the best way to go. Just hop on the bus.

I was also thinking of asking someone else. Someone that might actually appreciate the music for simply what it is. I was thinking of asking Kate, a girl that lives down the hall. It turns out that she applied to transfer to American also. It might be a good idea to invest some of my time into her. I mean, all year I've been thinking of really getting to know her. For some reason I've held back.

Kate is an interesting person. I don't want to go completely into it now, but I'll tell you what I think. On the surface, she comes off as completely normal and happy. It just seems so simple. Inside however, she's in pain. There are a lot of complex issues in her life. There is so much more to her, maybe even more than she knows. She, like me, is running from problems, by transferring. She's looking for love. She drinks and has sex to drown out her problems. She comes off as simple, but I know she is interesting, and I'd like to get to know the real her, behind the sex and the booze. I think she can help me as much as I can help her. Hopefully she'll go to the concert, and we'll have a chance to get to know each other.

11

For the first time in a long time, I feel like I finally accomplished something. I was accepted to American University, one of my original schools I wanted to apply to. So, after one year of hard work and determination, I made up for four years of soft performance in high school. This is getting me to thinking. Maybe things can go my way once in awhile, and maybe dreams are possible. It feels really good. Like I can go up to all the teachers whose classes I did bad in, my Dad and Karen, and everybody that thought I couldn't do it, and say, "you're wrong." It felt so great to tell my parents what my GPA was, and probably better to have them find out I got into American. This is for all the times that people told me that going to the schools I was thinking about was a pipe dream.

My work is not done, however. I need to finish out this semester strong, and do well at American. Then, I'll be able to transfer to either Chapel Hill or Duke. Duke is the prize. The moment I stepped onto the campus, it felt like home. I want Duke.

My Dad and I have to have a talk as soon as I get home. I need to let him know how I feel and he needs to know how I feel. When I came down here, it didn't matter the destination, only that it was a long way away from my family. I should start off by saying I love my family. I should follow that by saying they're really fucked up. I needed to get away from them, or they would have pulled me down with them. They're too far gone to clean. I can't do it. The best thing is for me to be disconnected from them.

This summer I don't want to be too connected. I want them to loosen the reins and leave me be. I want minimal interference. I realize this will probably never happen, knowing how screwed up they are, and how they're always trying to spite one another.

The last thing I want to briefly talk about is Maggie. I've been thinking about her a lot lately. Usually in bed, when I'm trying to sleep. I feel good about whatever happens this summer and in the future, I think things will work out between us, however it ends up.

April 6, 2000

12

Wow, I actually talked about it two times ago, so I need not press the issue. But I figure I should bring it up. It's the topic of asking Kate to go to the concert with me. It isn't the asking her that's the problem. Many times I've been misinterpreted about my intentions with girls. I don't want her to think of it as a date. I want to go as friends. I mean, we can see if anything is there, but I want her to know it's as friends first. Honestly, out of all the people down here, Kate is one of the few people I respect. Even though I might never see her again in eighteen days. I mean, if I don't ask her, my life will not be worth living. Even if she says no, which she very possibly will, at least I will know. If she says no, I have a couple uncomfortable moments with her, and the year is over. It's full proof. At nine – thirty I'll ask her. I hope she goes, because honestly, I don't want to go alone on the bus. Or at the concert for that matter. Wish me luck.

13

Well, I did it, and you can probably figure out the excuse. She didn't have any money. Too bad I couldn't help her out. All I really wanted to say is that I saw Bob Dylan tonight, and Hootie and the Blowfish yesterday. Dylan is amazing. He has a terrible voice, and I didn't know half of his songs, but he was great. He has an amazing presence. I am so glad I decided to live and went to this concert by myself. It kind of made me think of Maggie.

April 20, 2000

14

Usually there is a method to my madness. I usually have a profound reason as to why I write. Tonight, I do not. I found out that I have to take another train home and send my stuff parcel. Oh well. I was really hoping my Dad would come pick me up, but it turns out he didn't want to miss two days of work. Yeah, and Dave is back to shooting up. Twelve days before I come home, he starts shooting up.

This summer was supposed to be a time when we could make up for lost time due to his using drugs before. I was really excited about maybe working with him, and hanging out. He really let me down. I mean, it's an addiction, it's medical. I can't do anything about it and apparently neither can Dave. I'm not going to hold it against him. It's just frustrating. I'm also wondering about this summer. How's it really going to work out?

I talked the talk, about getting a car, living with mom, getting independence, and getting treated differently than in the past. I'd like to say I've made a lot of progress in one year, but I can't be sure.

The other question is, how is home going to be? Is the family shit going to be going on, like in the past? I think it will be, but I can't be sure. I have to tell my Dad that it's all shit. That it's all fucked up, and it's never going to get better. The fighting, the arguing, the utter chaos; it will never change. I need to tell dad that he chose that path, so he has to live with the shit, but I choose differently. I don't want to have the shit in my life. I love everyone in my family, but I don't like what all of them are doing. Note to self: if I come back to school here next year, I must get a girlfriend. Just not for sexual reasons, but because I need some support, emotionally. Looking at home, I at least have a support system there. Down here, I have no one. If it's only one person, I need them.

May 2, 2000

15

I left early this morning on a north bound train. Everything has changed... or has it? My mother moved closer to home, my brother stopped using drugs, and on the day I left, I professed my love for Maggie. This is the first time I will be home since all of these things have gone down.

There's some dispute too, as to where I will be attending college next year. Unless something dramatic happens this summer with Maggie, I'll be going back to UNCC for my fall semester. I know my parents want me to go to the University of Delaware, but that'll never happen.

Back to the subject, everything has changed since I was last home five months ago. I don't know what to expect when I get home. I'm expecting big things, a full time job, my own car, to live at my Mom's house, to continue to further develop my relationship with Maggie, and a more important part in my brother's life. This is what my ideal summer would look like. For some reason, I don't think my family will be able to let me meet these demands. I feel I've taken some big steps this year, being at school. I don't want to go home because I think my family will fuck it up for me. I love them all, but they're fucked up, and I don't think they will ever change. I'll find out shortly.

May 16, 2000

16

I've been home for two weeks and not much is going as planned. As soon as I got back, Dave began shooting up again. His friend overdosed, so Dave became depressed and started up again. Personally, I think he saw it as the perfect excuse to start doing drugs.

Something profound happened the other day with him. All day I was joking with my mom that I wanted to fight Dave, I mean, a real fist fight, punches and all. Later that night, my Dad, Dave and I were having a talk. I told Dave to knock off the drugs, or he would end up like his friend dead, and I told him I didn't want to have to go through losing him. It was the most serious I've been in awhile. Like a minute later he told me to fuck myself, so I stood up and said, "Do you want to fight?" We were about to fight when my Dad threw me back into a chair.

When we sat back down and resumed the conversation, I started crying. It was the first time in a long time I had cried. I think I was crying because this was the first time I realized how much pain Dave had actually caused me and the rest of my family. At that moment, I truly wanted to fight him, to hurt him. I mean, all the years I used to joke about drugs, like wasn't real until now, it finally hit me. So shit with Dave is all kinds of fucked up.

Let's move right along with something else that sucks, I've seen Maggie twice since I've been home, and again, I don't know what the deal is with us. That's definitely a bad sign. I want to speak briefly on what I like and dislike about Maggie. She amazes me. She's everything I'm looking for in someone I want to share myself with. She's so well-rounded, which is something I pride myself in, and admire. She's learning guitar, she's learning Italian. She is so smart and she likes to have a good time, and chill. That's exactly what I want. That's what I try to be like.

What I don't like though, is I think she is overextended. I think she has too much going on. I don't possibly see how she could share herself with me, when she has to give herself to so many other people and things. I want to be closer to her than everybody, except maybe her parents. I don't think I think like most people, I don't know. Well, I tried to explain to her how I wanted our relationship to go after Christmas. Maybe she doesn't understand me, or she just has too much other stuff going on to have that close of a relationship. Whatever the case, tonight was my last straw.

She fell asleep with me there, and that meant something to me. I know she was tired and she wanted to go to sleep. I totally understand that. I could have stayed up straight through the night until seven am and then gone into work, if I could be with her all night. I am simply stating that I think I care a lot more for her than she cares for me. It's called the principle of least interest: whoever has the least interest in a relationship has the most power. I don't think I can go on like this. I don't think I can just be her friend either. If I am going to be with Maggie I think it has to be all or nothing. I care too much about her to just sit around while she is off doing her thing. The entire population could fall off the face of the earth, as long as the two of us were here, it would be alright.

May 19, 2000

17

Wow, today is Thursday. Maggie called and left a message for me to call her before like seven-thirty pm, in other words, she was doing something with other people, which means to her, we are friends and only friends... I was going to attempt to have another conversation with her to sort things out, but that won't be necessary. I already know the answer. I haven't talked to her in about six months and I had all but forgotten about her. I wrote her off. Then, Tony happened to run into her this past fall. He asked her what ever happened between us, like why we didn't ever get together. She told him it was because I didn't show very much interest in her, but if I did, she would have gone through with it. This was all I needed to send me helplessly back in love with her.

I wrote her to see how she was doing. Over Thanksgiving, I honestly had one of the greatest nights of my life. It was as if all my hopes and aspirations about what I thought our relationship could be culminated in this one amazing night. Then, over Christmas, things went back to the old way. I was baffled. We talked several times and I assumed we would be separated when we were at school, but we'd be together when we were home. Obviously, her interpretation of our relationship is much more different than mine. I can pretty much say, with much assurance and confidence, that I'm just fucked. I'm in love with someone who likes me as a friend. I guess I'm just swimming up shit creek.

I believe the quote that there are three great women in every man's life. Now that I have successfully reaffirmed that I'm fucked, I think there's only one thing for me to do. I have to tell Maggie how I fucked up, and that I don't want to see her anytime soon. I need to get out on my own and put her out of my mind. It's the best thing for me.

June 7, 2000

18

The Sixers are in the NBA finals. I know it's not all that important in the overall grand scheme of life, but it feels good to get excited about something. Not since the '93 Phillies have I been this excited about professional sports.

It feels good. Babylon, by David Gray; that's the anthem for today.

I think tomorrow or the next day I will confront Maggie. I will confirm my belief that she does not love me, but only I am her friend. Once and for all, I need to have this end. I want to move forward. I want to make sure that going to University of Maryland is not the right thing to do. Once Maggie confirms my belief, I will be able to decide to stay at UNCC for one more year. I would go to the University of Maryland if Maggie gave me a reason to. You can talk all day about the academic differences, campus differences, and social life differences, but it ultimately comes down to one person. If she wants me to stay I will. If not, I will go out of her life forever. I feel bad though. I feel like she will have to make a decision without enough information. Maybe it was never going to work. I guess I'll never know.

June 8, 2000

19

In the past day, my opinion about Maryland has possibly changed. If I want to live that predictable life that everyone lives, I would stay at UNCC for another year. If I want to experience as much life as possible, I would probably go to Maryland. Now I'm thinking I'll go to Maryland for a year and then transfer after a year. I'm also thinking I'll go there even if Maggie doesn't want to have a deep relationship. I think I have to go for me, and not her, regardless. I'm not going to fail. For if I do, then my life will not be worth living.

I need to confront Maggie tomorrow night at the New Orleans café during dinner. If I do not, then I'll never know what could have been between us. If not for a misunderstanding, then my life will not be worth living. There are some things important in life, and that is one of them.

Tonight I noticed several things about Maggie while we watched a movie. She says the most obvious things that can go unsaid, they're just understood. Like, "That's gross." She also has the most adorable soft laugh. However pathetic this may sound, I just wanted to hold her in the movie theatre and tell her how sexy her laugh was. She also periodically glances over to see if you're paying attention or enjoying the movie. She is always waking me up when I fall asleep. I don't get her.

June 17, 2000

20

Oh my, what a difference a week makes. We're going out. After two years of countless struggles, frustration, and misunderstanding, I have finally accomplished what I said I was going to do after our prom. After the prom I wanted her. Fuck. This is all bullshit.

July 6, 2000

21

It happened for the first time ever tonight. I wanted to be somewhere else besides with Maggie. I choose to be with her and her friends instead of being with my own friends.

That isn't new. But what is new is the feeling I got after I made that decision. I didn't have a good night tonight and I knew that if I was with my friends, I probably would've had a good time. I'm in no way blaming Maggie, but rather, I blame myself. I felt bad selling my friends out like that. I promised Mike we would go bowling. He said that twice before when the two of us went out with Maggie we didn't do what we had originally set out to do. Tonight, I promised Mike that I would come through. I told him that if things didn't work out again I would never ask him to go with us again. And surprise, things didn't work out. Strike three, you're out.

Well then, I just feel like a big asshole. Even though I value my relationship with Maggie more than I value my friend's relationships, I don't think that tonight any significant contribution was made to our relationship. Instead of reminiscing about the old days with kids I didn't know, or even care to know, I could have been with my friends talking about things that I recall and experienced. This is the biggest reason for my bad mood.

Something else that I find interesting is the power of silence. Usually I'm in a great mood when I'm in Maggie's house, so I joke and talk a lot. But like I said, I wasn't happy tonight, so I rarely talked and didn't display my positive mood. I think this is the first time her family has seen me this way. The fact of the matter is that I'm actually a very sensitive person. I react to slight things. When I'm not in a good mood, I don't talk, and I do get depressed to a certain point. It's not hard to figure out if something is really bothering me. If it is bothering me enough I will act like this. Most stuff I'll let go though, by joking about it.

If Maggie really wants me, then she's going to have to take all of me. I'm not that unrelenting, sarcastic person that attempted to win her over. It was merely a façade, to hide what my real personality was. It is one aspect of my personality, but it's not nearly as big as when a person first meets me. I usually joke to hide something that is bothering me or to help myself take things less serious. If you take everything too serious, you will go crazy. The only things that you should be serious about are the things that truly matter and are important. Not much is worth being serious over.

July 18, 2000

22

Great, so now I'm going out with Maggie, my dream right? Well, no. It's the same old shit. When I told her I wanted to be on another level with her I meant it. I don't call hanging out with her family ever night to be on that level. I want to be real with her. I want to be with just her and have that amazing relationship with her that I told her about. Watching shitty movies with her family ever night isn't getting it done. Right now I'm crying. I'm so sad and angry. I have so much anger right now. I just want her to be able to see.

July 25, 2000

23

But now that the smokes gone, we can all see clear.

24

I am crying again. But they are tears of joy. I learned two very important things tonight. I love Maggie. And I can't change her or make her see. I will be attending the University of North Carolina for my sophomore year. Chasing after a girl by going to a different school was never the solution. After seriously flirting with the idea, it isn't the answer.

I love Maggie, and I'll continue to love her in North Carolina. I feel as if all the odds were stacked against us to have an amazing relationship, and with the weight of the world against us, we won, even if it was for a short while. I have always felt that our relationship was destined to fail. All I can do is give her all of my love and make this painful decision, because however hard it is to make right now, I know it will be for the best.

25

In my time of need I look to the pen to keep me awake and alive. It's one-nineteen in the morning, the day after I attempted to break up with Maggie. I told her that I loved her, but we couldn't be together because I was too frustrated and angry that I couldn't change her. I realized something, however. Maybe the reason I can't change, no, fuck it.

August 10, 2000

26

It's been awhile since I have last written, but my thoughts remain constant.

August 11, 2000

27

If I could be like that, well I'd give anything. Well, it appears this Maggie thing is finally over with. It's hard to image. For so long now it's just been her. If I can bring one thing out of this experience, it's that now I know what it is like to be in love. I guess I also know what it's like to break off a relationship. Even though I know it was the right thing for me to do, it hurts so badly. The thing that hurts the most is that we can't remain friends, or talk to each other. That hurts. Why does she have to be that way? Well, my life moves on from here. But like the quote, what doesn't kill you, only makes you stronger.

August 12, 2000

28

I want to start a band. I've put it off long enough. It feels like time is running out on this idea of mine. I've been thinking about it for awhile, but now I feel like it's time to act on it. I think when I go to Maryland next month, I'll ask around. I would have to be the lead singer. I can't play any instruments, so I would have to sing. I don't think I have the greatest voice, but I do think I have soul.

I would probably want to cover songs at first, and then make our own. I love to sing, so this should be good. Before I had said I just wanted to concentrate on my school work and see Maggie on the weekends. Since the Maggie thing hasn't worked out, I should have time to make a band. If I get a girlfriend too, that would be alright.

I can't put so much faith in a girl right now. At least for awhile. I put too much faith in Maggie, I wanted so much for her to see things my way, but when she couldn't, I was crushed. I put so much energy and thought into her and it turned out we were not and never will be on the same page. However hard it is for me now, I know it's for the best. What I'm worried about is, no one sees things my way. I guess from now on I can look for it in a girlfriend, but I can't let it be the only thing and take control. As long as they support me, I should be alright.

August 14, 2000

29

I realized something at work today. I saw so many guys who have completely wasted their lives working. I'm not implying that people shouldn't work; only that work shouldn't consume someone's life. Like, time goes by so quickly, and when you finally stop to look around, you're 50 years old, and you haven't done shit with your life.

For instance, take John Collins, who works at the Waja warehouse. I was joking with him today about how I felt sorry for him, and in a way, I do. Here's a man who has worked his ass off his entire life and what is the highlight of his life this year; a one week trip to Busch Gardens, with his wife who he probably hates and his kids who he resents. It just isn't right. He's a good worker and deserves better.

Tomorrow is a very important day for me, even though I may not realize it. Tomorrow I talk to my dad about my living arrangements this year and if I have a car down at school. I see no reason why, never mind, it'll be tough, but I must stand my ground.

30

Here's what I feel in a song.
"Dark and Damned"
I just wanted us to be free
Stand at the edge of the earth
Clinging to each other
I just wanted you to see
You and I were all that would matter
Hardened and blinded
My penultimate plea
The outcome became obvious
Crying became obsolete
You couldn't hear all the clatter
Join, I pleaded with an outstretched hand
Feel my pain, feel my love
You and me till forever
Nothing else matters
You saw my pain but felt none yourself
Feeling my love you gave none yourself
Trying to avoid the inevitable
I lay in my bed
Questioning everything I hold true
Pain lying with every question I ask
You couldn't see
Why should I resist
What I want does not exist

August 19, 2000

31

Today is actually the unofficial last day I'll ever see Maggie. It ended much unlike how it began. We exchanged items that belonged to each other. We asked each other when we were going back to school. Then there was an awkward silence. As the odds that she was going to speak first dwindled, I decided to walk out with some respect as I said "See ya." I turned back to my car, got in, and left.

Of course like I expected, I returned to the house and cried hysterically for two minutes before my friend called me. I feel good and bad about what I did. Good because I followed through with my original plan, and because I was the one who ended it. I said see-ya before we got a chance to talk which has its flip side.

I don't know if I should attempt to contact Maggie and finalize the issue. I might do that, because she gave one of her CD's by accident. For the two seconds, it looked like she wanted me to talk to her, tell her what I was feeling, like normal, but this time I just left. I said fuck it. If she really cared about me, she would have called. I have a lot I could say to her but I don't know if it would serve a valid purpose. In the end, I don't think she cares enough. I can't wait to get back to school!

August 20, 2000

32

Hopefully this will be a short entry because I just want to talk about aspect of my relationship with her. I told her that I really wanted to know her and I wanted her to know me. I was upset because she couldn't break through her barriers of conventional behavior. She saw me as just another guy or boyfriend. The fact of the matter is, I wanted to be closer than two people have ever been. To accomplish this there needs to be a clear line of communication, complete honesty.

4

The University of North Carolina at Charlotte: Fall Semester, Sophomore Year

August 25, 2001

33

Well, this is the first time I'm writing since I've been back at school. It won't be that long. I just wanted to get it out. Since I've been back, I think the phrase cautiously optimistic, or maybe pessimistic optimism can be used. I think things will go better this year. And I'll have more experiences, but there's no way to tell. It's early and if I learned anything last semester, it's you can't pass judgment too early.

Since I've been back down here, I've seen a lot of girls that interest me, but I think I'm going to take a different approach this time. Instead of trying to find that perfect person, that sees the "Big Picture," right now, instead I think I need to live it up for awhile. The fact is most girls, or people for that matter don't understand the big picture. I think I held it against people last year. I can't do that now. I need to experience life, and accept people for who they are. I mean, that's what I did to Maggie. Essentially, I broke up with her because she didn't see or understand there's a bigger picture. That wasn't right. I love her, and I fucked things up with her. Granted, she did some strange things like bring her mom bowling and things like that. The fact is, I love her despite that. I think I tried to get too deep, too soon. What is it two months? I still miss her.

Over Christmas I think I will see if we can still be friends or all I know is that when I take off after I graduate, she's welcome to be right next to me. In fact, I want her there. If she could understand and support me in my personal belief that there is more out there, that would be enough for me. So if I hold it together, this should be a good school year.

August 27, 2001

34

Well, I guess my plan for dealing with Maggie didn't last. Turns out I sent her a one page email, which she might not ever get. It contained my thoughts about her. I basically said I shouldn't have broken up with her because she doesn't see things my way in terms of a bigger picture in life. It wasn't fair and I regret it. Now, why I was an asshole to her in Tom Jones was a different story. I told her she needs to work on her communication. I said when I wrote her the letter I wanted her to respond. When she didn't respond it angered me. I apologized and again asked her to talk to me. My point may have been moot. Of late, I can't stop thinking about her. I want to at least talk to her again. I've signed up for counseling sessions through the school. I'm excited about it. I think these can really help me. Please have her respond to me.

August 28, 2001

35

Well, maybe another chapter in my life has been closed. My prayer was answered. Maggie responded and I called and talked to her. Bottom line, she didn't want a boyfriend now, and our distance didn't help things. Had she wanted more, I honestly would have transferred to Maryland spring semester.

Move on. Put her on the back burner. Look for somebody else. These are things people have told me to do. They say why aren't you happy? I mean, at least you're on speaking terms with her. My response would be this. My experiment or way of thinking has failed me. I love Maggie, but I also wanted to have that amazing relationship with her. I wanted her to let it all go; all that stuff that doesn't matter, if I could have just gotten her to put it behind her. Was it fair of me to expect her to change her whole way of thinking and let it go? Probably not, but the fact remains I am disappointed. Great, I'm crying now. This is basically the deal. Everything else besides this doesn't matter. I broke up with Maggie because I realized I couldn't change her thinking. I still want to find someone who can let it all go, but in the process, I fell in love with Maggie. I would transfer to Maryland second semester to be near her, because I'm in love with her. All she had to say was she wanted to try to work things out. I made it clear that if it would take time, I would be in it for the long haul. She said she didn't want to go out with anybody. We'd still be friends. At least I finally got her to be honest. The truth is the only thing that ever helped anybody anyway. I guess I'm so upset because I found out the girl I love, doesn't want to go out with me. It hurts.

The thing about it is, deep down, I always knew I was more into her, than she was into me. The whole thing was destined for failure. After the prom, she hurt me. I really liked her and she never called me back. Is it suppose to hurt this much?

So by chance, when I saw her in the movie theatre, she invited me to call her, so we could do something. At that moment I made a promise to myself that I would pursue her until she told me she wasn't interested. I was dead set on doing this, so she would have to be in that position. I wanted to put her on the spot and feel bad about doing it. I wanted her to feel guilty because when she never called me back, she really hurt me.

I can remember throwing empty Wendy's cups out the window of the van at her house. I also promised myself that I would never get too deeply involved with her, so when I finally got her to do it, I got deeply hurt. It's funny, because since I've known her, or after that movie night, I realized it would end like this, and it still hurts so much. You might think because I knew, it would be better. I mean for two years now, off and on, Maggie has been my interest.

In my short adult life, I know no other serious interest. On the eve of opportunity I think fear has surrounded me. Fear of the unknown. Fear of not being able to say, oh yeah Maggie my girlfriend, or yeah Maggie, I'm to go out with her. Fear of having no one. What if I don't meet anybody? There are a whole bunch of questions with very few answers. The answers to my questions can only come with time. With the day that comes tomorrow. So, in time, all of my questions will be answered.

Back to things I can answer. My therapist appointment is tomorrow and I strongly look forward. Maybe there some of my questions will be answered. One thing I did notice, I came down to North Carolina because the people are nice, friendly, and the weather is nice, well that's not half the reason, but they did add into the final equation. What I figured is that maybe I needed to go to Boston to be around northern people. Only because I have a strange notion they might be deeper. I don't know. Just a thought.

September 10, 2001

36

Nothing much is new, but I just felt like writing. Wow, I suddenly just recapped my summer, and in just thinking about it, it didn't seem that shitty. I know all that shit happened with Maggie, and with Dave, and even not seeing my dad too much. But I was thinking about working at Waja, and I looked at it as a positive experience. I now look ahead to this year with cautious optimism. I think maybe two weeks ago, I had a feeling of despair, but now I feel better.

One of my roommates, Azar, has been a friend to me. He's invited me several times to do things with him. It's like, at least there's somebody else to hang out with. I also noticed something tonight. I compared my friends back home to my ones here, and I realized something. With the exception of J-Will, I don't ever feel too comfortable around anybody. Ok, with the exception of Eryn too, but that's a different story. Like, for instance, when playing pool back home, I always joke around. I'm bad, I know it, and when I play I don't give a fuck. When Azar and I played tonight he was telling me to concentrate, and when I distracted him he told me seriously not to distract him. That's the difference. When I play pool with my friends back home, we don't give a fuck, we just go play to have fun, and we surely don't coach each other. For the most part, our philosophy is if it goes in, good, if not, maybe next time.

Down here I always have my guard up. I don't like revealing myself to people unless I can trust them and I think they're quality people. So far, yet again, with maybe the exception of J-Will, I haven't met any quality people. I mean, I just want to get real with somebody. Like when Azar is telling me about how his car's getting five more horse power, I just want to say to him, so who gives a fuck. Like when he bumps that soft R&B shit, I just want to tell him no, and when I meet a kid like Trent, and all he talks about is getting high or drunk, I want to say DRUGS! Like Bigas and I used to; tell him to get a life. Like when I hear motherfuckers that are so wrapped up in their insignificant lives, I just want to be real with them. I want to meet some people that can take a step back, take things easy, loosen up, and I want to say to them what I'm really thinking. Azar thinks I'm shy, I just don't know how to talk to him, or other people like him.

September 11, 2001

37

September 11,, 2001, a date which will live in infamy. I'll try not to be so dramatic, but today terrorists crashed planes into the World Trade Center, and the Pentagon, and some field in Pittsburgh area. My dad said that this is the most important political event that has happened in his entire life. For him to say that, he's lived through a lot of shit. And while this is so important, I want to talk about something a little different.

Some girl who my roommate had hung out with a couple of times before came over. When she had come over before I got, well, let me say she was alright looking. When I hung out with her before I got the impression she didn't have much going on upstairs. Well, long story short, she came over drunk, and basically he fucked her. Although maybe I shouldn't, I have several different thoughts and feelings on the issue. At first I thought, lucky him, then I got a little jealousy, then I thought to myself, why am I feeling these things. I mean sure I want to fuck, but a girl like that. Every time I've seen this girl, she's either high or drunk. I guess a fuck is a fuck, but something disturbs me about the whole thing.

If I'm having sex with a girl, I must deeply care for her, if not love her. I just don't think I can have it otherwise. That's why I wanted to have sex with Maggie. I am in love with her and it would have been her first time. But now that won't happen, at least anytime soon. That means I must find someone who I care about. My mom says I'm a catch. I'm popular.

September 12, 2001

38

Even though I have other things on my mind, I want to address one thing. The terrorists; I think when they died they were under the impression that they have an afterlife with forty virgins. I have news for them. They're wrong.

39

I have some studying I can be doing, but when I went to the psychologist and she asked me to answer a question. The question is: why do I care what other people think? And I've been trying to figure out why. J-Will suggested that it is if I let people see the real me, they will pass judgment on me, and they will see that I'm not as great as I think I am. Like I said, I think I am the greatest, but I don't think others will see me that way. This might be true, but I'm not so sure.

The way I'm seeing things right now, my life is a complete contrast. On one hand, my outward self, I seem completely normal. I have normal friends, I do pretty well in school, I work part-time, I was on the football and basketball teams, I was always a polite kid, and I never got into trouble. On the outside, I am what one might call your standard, good, successful kid. My life contrasts in a more internal way. Although I symbilify all these things above, internally I dismiss most of them. There's a deeper, much more different me, that I let out to a few people.

For instance, I think differently from my friends. I don't think doing well in school means much of anything. People get treated so much differently. I was on our school basketball team. That's the biggest sign of brainwashing. I didn't believe in the cause. I think most people are petty. There are few important things and most people are enveloped in the things that don't matter. I think my problem is this. The world I live in is run by these people. Like, I'm proud to be an American.

I think the recent terrorist attacks aren't as important as some like to think. Simply, violence provoking terrorists should all die so equilibrium can be restored. So I must conform to society, until the right time comes when I can deviate. Right now I am playing a role. I don't want to screw it up before the time is right. Maybe for credibility later do I care if I am judged normal by others. I think I need her direction to help me find the answer.

September 28, 2009

40

After talking to the psychologist, I realized it's important to find out when in my life, or in the process, do I care what other people think. For instance, when I'm with Bigas and he's acting like a jackass in the car, why do I get upset and care? Because I know people see what I'm doing. They probably look down at me and think I'm a jackass. Bigas doesn't care, I do. Why? If a cop pulls me over for being obnoxious, I care, Bigas doesn't, and I care what the cop thinks about me.

October 5, 2001

41

Wow, its three-twenty am on a Friday night/Sat morning. I can't go to sleep because the people who live next door to me are fucking, and I can't fall asleep with people moaning. I also have an idea.

I don't think I ever write about J-Will, but I think I should write more about him. He is fascinating. This year it seems like he trusts me more, and I'm getting to open up more and try new things. Like tonight we went to a volleyball match, and last week we went to a concert. Last year I couldn't get him to go to either thing.

I am also thinking about something else. I think it's time I get over Maggie. I mean, I still love her, but with the entire situation looking bleak, and getting bleaker, I need to experience some things. I wanted to experience life with her, and I wanted everything to be with her, but it looks like that won't happen so I think it's time. I think it's time I find a girl counterpart to J-Will. I mean, someone who I can just be completely honest with, someone who will get me, and someone I can have sex with. I want to care for someone else. This time, however, I can't pull a "Maggie" and fuck it up. I have to move on, I can't let life pass me by, I need to make a stand, and live.

I want to talk about my roommates Azar and Alem. I don't understand them, and it's for the worse. They come off as though they are God's gift to the world. They love talking about themselves, more so, than anybody I've ever met. They love telling me about how great they are and how much they know. It might be cultural or genetic, I don't know. But it poses a problem. I think tomorrow I will talk to Azar about it. Plus, they make fun of J-Will, which pisses me off. I got to be honest with them. I'm going to tell them that J-Will stays in his room because he thinks they are pieces of shit because the way they act, thinking they're top shit. I, on the other hand, think it might be cultural, or they're genetically like that, but they have two options. The first is stop making fun of J-Will and leave him alone. The second is attempt to befriend him, and not be dicks about it. I assume they'll choose number one.

To change the subject, I submitted my first article to the newspaper, it might be printed on Thursday, and I am really excited. For the first time I will have shared my thoughts on something publically. I can't wait to see the response, unless they want to kill me. I think I might be happy.

October 7, 2001

42

I just had a good conversation with Mike and it was good. He told me that he actually met a girl that might be interested in him, and I tried to talk him through how to develop things. It always seems like I can give great advice, but when it comes to me, I don't have much of a clue. I didn't want to write much, just that. Maybe I should meet more people.

October 13, 2001

43

I guess I want to complain about my roommate right now. Both of the foreigners. They think they're so great. Tonight, Azar took me to Jillian's to play pool. I went, not because I like him particularly much or because I'm good or even I like pool, but because I didn't want to spend Friday night home alone.

Okay, so we get to the place and we start playing, and of course I lose. I rarely play pool, and when I do it's just for fun and I usually lose. So of course I get my ass beat, but I'm a good sport. Then we go to some kid's house and play foozball. Of course I've never played before, so I sucked. It was alright until the kids made some comments about me sucking, all in fun of course, but it still annoyed me. After that, I played Azar in some boxing video game he always plays, and he beat my ass. So I took some time off. Through all of this I have been a good sport.

So finally, I get Azar to play me in a basketball video game, something I'm a little familiar with. But of course, I double up his score and beat the living shit out of him. The whole game, as he's sucking, he complains about how the game is bad. He really sucks and it felt great to beat him. He always wins because everything we compete at, he is very experienced in. Then, tonight he tried to brag about having a big screen TV with surround sound. It felt so good to tell him I have the same thing. Then he tried to say his TV was as big as the sofa. What a fucking joke! That kid is a fucking joke.

October 16, 2001

44

I always thought when I got myself into a situation, one that I really believed in, it would work out. You know, things would go my way. Like maybe things were scripted out for me. I'm not suggesting that God has a plan for me, merely that for whatever reason, my life was scripted. The last few months, I've felt like this is not the way it was supposed to go. Maybe it is, but it doesn't feel right. One choice changed everything. Or maybe it just put me back on track. Back where I should be. Maybe it's working itself out, it's just hard to see right now.

October 31, 2001

45

Today is Halloween, but that is not why I'm writing. A lot of bad things have happened the pass two days, and I guess I just wanted to bitch about that. I don't know. I know I felt really sad tonight, though. I had just gotten finished watching Dawson's Creek, in which Dawson's dad died and it was all depressing. Then, I went into J-Will's room to tell him how depressing it was, and he threw a chair at the ground because Vince Carter didn't get a foul called for him. I was then even more depressed after this and I headed to the library. On the way there I almost started to cry, and I don't think I know why. Actually, I might have an idea. I think it's because I had death on my mind, then J-Will getting pissed over a stupid game reminded me that no matter how close you are to one person, you can never understand them or agree with them completely. Then, this all made me think about Maggie. Then I started debating about whether or not I should try to see her this winter. I still don't know. But as one can see, all of this stuff sucks, a great deal. I just hope it turns out alright.

November 2, 2001

46

I just wanted to write tonight too clear my head so I can study statistics. Well, this is a good song on Live at the

World Café, good songwriter song. All trying to be Joan Baez. Well, let's see. I'm trying to nail Dave's ex-girlfriend. From what I hear, she's cute. She also seems to be nice. She does seem to be not so intelligent. It appears she had a rough childhood, her father is in jail and her mother is a waitress. She lives in Marcus Hook, and that's kind of a white trash neighborhood. I think she had sex with Dave and they only knew each other for two weeks. I figure I have a pretty good shot. I wouldn't leave her like Dave though. I think that was cruel. She would be something to come home to. Of course I am speaking without having met her, formally, maybe she'll suck too much and I won't get involved, or maybe, although not very likely, I'll fall in love with her, and she wouldn't just be someone to come home. If I choose to not get involved she seems to be the perfect case study. Maybe I could find out what she's thinking, or not thinking. The seventh game of the World Series is on and I've got five bucks on the Diamondbacks. I want to be a rock star and I don't know what I want to do with Maggie.

November 4, 2001

47

For those about to rock, we salute you. Tomorrow morning, I have to go to the psychologist. I don't know what we're going to talk about, so I thought it might be good if we discussed. Not to overdo it, but maybe my near obsession with Maggie could be talked about. I know I shouldn't still be thinking about her, but for some reason. Then in a somewhat related topic, in the future or present, how willing will I be to give my entire self to somebody. I just want it to be done the right way this time. Although I say I want normalcy, when was normalcy fun. It would actually be a change for me. When am I going to let people be good enough for me around here. Like I don't even give them a chance, I just write them off. When will I open myself back up, because I was open in the past. I've grown more closed the last few years. I need some inspiration.

November 7, 2001

48

I'll write until I can't anymore. I just saw some statistics that said eighty percent of all people have sex before the age of twenty. I didn't know it was so high. Well, it's twelve-thirty in the morning, and I thought I felt like writing. I guess I'll write about the girl I met today. I was waiting for my professor during his office hours and so was she, with her roommate. We talked for about ten to fifteen minutes. After I had my appointment, she was still waiting, so I exchanged names with her.

I should have asked her out, but I didn't. I don't know what stopped me from doing it. I mean she was fairly attractive, and we held a pretty fluid conversation. So I guess here's where I tell you about her. She had long blonde hair, thin to medium, average breasts... She had a cute Southern accent. I mean the entire situation was ideal. She was a Freshman, she lived in a crowded high rise dorm (Moore), she told me that she didn't party very much, she was undecided about a major and needed some guidance, she was even thinking about majoring in child psychology. The situation seemed ideal. She seemed like she was interested in me. The only road block would be if she had a boyfriend, but that might not even be a problem. So why did I stall out? I mean, I shook her hand, we exchanged names, all I had to do was say, "So, would you like to get together sometime, or would you want some help with psychology?" That's all. I stopped myself because in my mind I didn't want to act like an asshole. But I need to stop that foolish thinking. I need to start living. This is where it starts.

November 9, 2001

49

And I suppose it was. This is where I take back the power. Well, actually, I did do something noteworthy; at least for me. Tonight I asked out some girl. She works at Burger King and she is Bosnian. Turns out she has a boyfriend. Oh, well, at least I did it. I am actually kind of relieved now that I did it.

I was kind of down on myself since really the whole Maggie fiasco. I guess today, is like the day I moved on. Get on with my life. I don't want to blow this out of proportion; I mean after all, I did get shot down. It sucks too because she was nice looking. She also had a pretty good personality. It is good though, that before I came home to face my demons, I took a step forward.

There's only one thing to do now. Use this new found courage and keep moving forward. Like my mom said, for every ten that say no, one will say yes. I'm going home this week for Thanksgiving. I have mixed feelings about going home. I mean I don't want to fly because of all of the shit going on recently, but I guess it would be okay to see my family. I mean I haven't seen them in over three months. I hope the trip home is all well and I keep the ball rolling.

November 28, 2001

50

Well, I am back at school. I never thought I would actually say it, but I like that "control" song. Yeah, well Thanksgiving kind of sucked, but at least I finished that research paper. This weekend I finally told dad that I didn't like coming home. I told him I am sick of all the shit going on and I don't want to be around it. I think it brings me down.

On my own, I have control and I determine my future. Around Dad's house, though, I don't feel in control because I think mentally they control me. Whether I am actually controlled is in question, I definitely feel the pressure of their control. So I talked to Dad about it, but I need to talk to Karen about it over Christmas. Karen told me that she thinks I have a great amount of anger and resentment towards her, I don't know if this is true. I do have anger. I think I need to find the source of this. I also have pain, although I'm not sure why.

I don't know if I have written this previously, but I have been thinking of this recently. Of course it's about Maggie. I realize now why I broke up with her. I completely overanalyzed the whole situation. I broke up with her because I felt very strongly for her. Whether it was true or not, I felt as if I cared much more for her than she cared about me. This made me feel vulnerable, and exposed. I had more to lose than her. As a result

I ended it with the assumption that at some point it would fail sooner, rather than later. The longer I let it drag on, the more exposed I would have made myself. I didn't want to experience this hurt or rejection because I was experiencing it already for only the short time that we went out. I over thought my reasoning looking for intellectual reasons or philosophical reasons to justify our split, when in actuality the reasons were much simpler, they were emotional reasons. Essentially, I wanted to give my entire self to her and wanted her entire self. She did not give me her entire self so I felt rejected, and this hurt me.

So what is next? With Maggie that is? The truth is, I don't know, I do know this, I think over Christmas we need to talk. I need to tell her what I've written above. I then should apologize for the way things worked out, and for criticizing what little she did disclose to me. I must then assure her that I like the whole her, all faults considered. What I should do after this is still up in the air. I guess at this point I could do a thousand different things. The best of these things I could possibly do might be to just walk away. Maybe, at this point I have done all I can do concerning this girl, and if things are going to continue she needs to want them to. It would then be up to her to approach me. Relationships are a two-way street. She will then either approach me or not approach me, depending on how much of herself she wants to give to me. I have given all I can up until this point.

November 30, 2001

50

I cut myself just to feel alive, no I don't really, but I cut into this acne to get the puss out, it always gets big and red, and is an eyesore on my face. I hate it. It has been going on for over five years now, this acne. I'm a good looking kid if I didn't always have all this shit on my face. I hate it and I think to some degree it has affected my development of social skills. People don't find acne attractive. I don't find it attractive. It has plagued me for some time now and I don't know what to do. I've tried everything. I've even resorted to using toothpaste recently. Nothing works. I feel embarrassed when I go out in public. I think that people look down upon me because of my acne. It is making me crazy. I talked to the shrink today and she agreed that I am angry at Karen, and at home in general. I have had to go through some serious argumentative stuff where I have been put in the middle. This certainly contributes to me being angry at Karen, and home in general. There is a lot of anger.

December 8, 2001

51

Black is a good song, I like it. My mom just called and told me I was getting a nose job over spring break for a Christmas present. I can't really argue with that. Right now though, I have Finals week. Starting tomorrow is hell week. I have four finals this coming week. If I do well on them, I could finish up with a good GPA. If I do well

I'll probably get into Chapel Hill. Then it really begins. I think I'll do well. I was also talking to Chris Neeb about starting up this band. It appears that Chris and I are the only members so far. He'll play acoustic guitar and I'll sing. We have decided to have three songs ready for Christmas break. The three songs are Layla, Polley, and Desperately Wanting, but I think I might change that to, This Time of Year. I look forward to our playing.

I would also like to note that I am seriously considering joining Spencer's frat, if it is only for one semester. I know I talk a lot of shit about frats, but it will give me some social life. It'll make second semester go by quicker.

December 14, 2001

52

Unabashed honesty would be ideal, but like a prophet did once say, honesty is a lonely word. I know I talked yesterday, but there is a matter of importance I would like to discuss. It would be that one small matter with Karen. Well I'm going to the psychologist tomorrow, so we can address it then. Karen wrote me an email essentially explaining to me that she wasn't paying for the remainder of the tuition. She said that I will have to sue my mom for the rest of the money. She then proceeded to tell me all of the things she thought I should have been doing, half of which I have done on my own. I feel controlled because of that. I wanted to be responsible and get my job back over break without being told. But of course, she told me to in the email. I don't like it. I need a resolution.

5

The University of North Carolina at Charlotte: Spring Semester, Sophomore Year

53

I know it must not seem this way, but I have begun to move past Maggie. I took a big step tonight. Tonight, J-Will and I hung out with Michele, the girl who lives upstairs. At the beginning of the night it appeared as though she was interested in me. But as the night progressed to a point I thought she was more interested in J-Will. I don't know what to make of her. One thing did stand out about her which I liked. She said she moved from New Jersey to North Carolina to be near her boyfriend. Of course, she just broke up with her boyfriend. But that shows me she's willing to take a risk. I am like that. I almost transferred to Maryland to be near Maggie.

I think I'm going to go to group therapy. I need to continue to figure out who I am. I mean, tonight I was completely sarcastic, and that's how I act when I first meet a girl, because I want them to find me unique and want to differentiate myself from every other guy. I don't want to be just any guy, even thought I very well might be. I think I'm great, and I can be better and more enlightened than others, but what if I'm wrong. What if I'm not great. What then? And I'm looking man, I'm looking. I'm still trying to find that perfect girl. That person that I can totally know, and I look at every girl I meet and think, maybe this is her. I don't want to fall for someone, or think they're the girl, unless they really are. I set myself up with Maggie and got hurt. I wanted someone so much that I had her assume a role that she is incapable of filling. I don't want to do this with anyone else. Only thing is, I told Maggie what I wanted and she was unresponsive.

I think I know what I want to do with Michele. I think I'll make an attempt to be real with her and try to go out sometime. Nothing sexual, just as friends, I want to see what this girl is all about. It sounds like she's been through a lot and maybe I could help her out while learning about myself in the process. I will ask her if she would like to talk about her break up because it seems as though she has no one close to her down here, and we all can use a friend.

January 20, 2002

54

I just want to write. I'm kind of angry right now and I just want to write. I'm backed into a wall and there's no way out. I like being alone, but not all the time. I think I might be fucked if I don't act quickly. I want several things for this semester. I want to get a 4.0. I want to build up my body through bench press. I want to get a job. And I want to meet that person. Right now I have none of them. I want them. I'm afraid I have lost or will lose the companionship of J-Will here my last semester. So for five months I'm going to have to do it on my own.

January 26, 2002

55

It's twelve thirty-seven on Monday night. I need to sleep because I have two new classes tomorrow, and a full schedule. First though, I must record what I am thinking and feeling. I've been lying here in the dark for about forty minutes trying to sleep. Then, Raining in Baltimore, by the Counting Crows came on. And I remember. God my life could have been so different. I just pictured this one night, and how my decision literally changed my life. Over the summer, I was over Maggie's house. I fucked it up. It was late at night and only her grand mom was home. We were watching a movie at her house. We were sitting on the couch. We started kissing and then I suggested we fool around. At first she was hesitant because her grandmother was upstairs, but we proceeded. We did this for awhile and then stopped. Before we began though, she suggested we wait until Wednesday and go to her apartment. I insisted we not wait. This is where I went wrong. My whole life changed in that instant. I never said I regret anything in my life before, but I regret this. I should have told her that we should go to her apartment the next day. I would make her dinner, then we could be alone. Also, if I had questions about her commitment to me, I should have asked her about it. Instead of being extreme and dumping her.

You know, because I'm thinking about it now, and I think she did like me. I mean, she let me fool around with her. I remember that night she wore that really tight "Class of 2000" tee-shirt because I asked her to. I remember she took me to her old house, and let me into her past. I suck. What the fuck was my problem. Here's this girl. I really like, she likes me, but I'm so blind I don't see it and I act like an asshole. It felt so good with her. But it wasn't good enough for me. Shit. I want her back. And it hurts. I tried talking to her over break and she ignored me like I didn't exist. I think I fucked this one up big-time.

February 9, 2002

56

It's only ten forty-five now, so I should be able to get to bed earlier tonight in time for Intro to Psychology. Well, I think I figured some things out. I was going to leave after I wrote my last thoughts. I was going to go to Baltimore this weekend. I was going to just show up. Yeah, unannounced; I don't think that's a good idea now. I just emailed Maggie to see if she wanted me to come up to talk. I won't go if she doesn't write back.

I learned something even more important today. I am a perfectionist. I hold myself to a high standard. I have to be better than everybody else. Then, when I have looked for friends, but especially a girlfriend, I hold people to such a high standard. I basically set myself and others up for failure. I am looking for that perfect person, that diamond in the rough, that person that doesn't exist. It's like I wanted it so badly that I made Maggie this person, and when she couldn't live up to it, as inevitably she never would be able to, I was angered. I felt rejected and well that's it. So basically I have to realize that I'm not better than everybody else. And yes, maybe I analyze more than many people, but that doesn't make me any better. And I'm going to have to stop looking for the female form of me. She doesn't exist.

Yes, I try to be a Renaissance man. I try to be elite in my thinking and all aspects of life. Well shit, J-Will thinks that all people, including him, aren't shit. We make fun of those people who actually think they're somebody. I think most people aren't shit, but there a few, including myself, that are worth something. I also make fun of those people who think they're somebody when they are not. I also think I'm afraid of disappointment, but first, sleep beckons me.

February 10, 2002

57

It's Friday night or Saturday morning, depending on how you look at it. I thought I was going to meet the person tonight, but all I did was see Eryn. I saw her at the movies. I just kind of nodded and walked away. I felt good afterwards though. Not to think too highly of myself, but I know I looked good tonight. She looked her normal unattractive self. What is it with me and seeing people from the past at the movies?

I just want to find an average girl. Looks aren't as important to me as the quality of the relationship. I just want to know somebody, accepting them, and have somebody know me, and accept me. My mom told me in a letter that in time all good things will come to me. I hope she's right.

February 20, 2002

58

Well, I got a job and I worked all weekend. I'm very proud of myself for doing this. This was the first job I have ever gotten on my own accord. I bus tables, but hey, it's money. I was a man about the situation. My dad told me he was going to stop sending me money. When I ran out of money, I got a job. I did what I had to do, to survive. I don't want to give myself too much credit, but I think this is great. This job will give me something to do on the weekends. It will also help me meet people. I've already met many people there. Most of them seem decent enough, and many go to school with me. This is also a great way to meet girls. Either the one's working there or one's that come in. There are several girls that are fairly attractive to decent. In particular there's two girls that stuck out to me today. One of these girls was checking me out. She is kind of thick, but she looked decent. The other girl has big eyes and is tall, but besides that I'd say she's hot. Again, several other girls there, but I haven't met them. I look forward to next weekend when I can start to get to know the different people.

February 24, 2002

59

I don't want to skim the surface. I had a great feeling and idea today. Today was just one of those days where you put it all together. I figured out what I wanted to do with my life. I want to change the world. No, literally, I single handedly want to change the world. I want to be like Gandhi, or Martin Luther King, even bigger. I basically want to change the world from the way it exists today. Primarily I want to change the world economy to make the world more equal. I don't know how I'm going to do this, or what will be put in place. I just know I want to change it. I want to abolish religion. This seems to be a formidable task. I must study this all more in depth so that I can come up with better solutions.

March 3, 2002

60

Every once in awhile I write about my girl status, I think I'll do that. I finally got over the hump with the whole Maggie thing. The other night I made out with the make out slut. Then, I stood Mandy up on the next night, saw her at a club, and played it off. It was great. So I'm back in the game as they say. It took me awhile, but I'm back.

This semester I'm trying to be more social. I want to be in the "making friends" trend when I transfer, so my transition will be easier. Anyway, I have been going out with Spencer more so maybe I can meet people through him.

I also got a job, which has been okay. The money is pretty good, but I can't make out who's available at the restaurant. I mean, in terms of the girls. I've only been working there a week or so, so maybe it's too soon. Anyway, there are several perspectives. The one on the top of the list is this girl I met today, Jessica. She's a little blonde girl, real cute, she goes to school with me. She seems to be really upbeat, like she's on speed, she also mentioned she writes poetry which can only be a plus. When I first met her I thought she was really into me, but after awhile I realized that she is just naturally friendly, and smiles at most people. I mean, off the bat, this girl seems like my best bet. Of course I need to talk to her more, find out if she's available, if she's interested, and all the rest. I met this other girl, Rachel tonight. She was cute in her own right, and pretty thin. I noticed she whined and complained a lot like a nag. She was, however, very sarcastic, which I am, so that's good. I don't know about me. I like my women to be able to rough it up a little bit, she seemed high maintenance. A plus is that she is my age and goes to school with me. There are several other prospects, but these 2 seem the most likely from a distance. I guess only time will tell.

March 7, 2002

61

Today I had my first encounter with organized government, not including me voting in the US election last year. I officially became the Arts and Sciences representative for UNCC. This is my first political position. I want to do it so that I can learn how the government works. If possible, I also want to see how my philosophies match up with the way things work. First impressions: It seemed like most of the people in government are assholes. For the entire two and a half hour meeting it seemed as though they were hung up on little, unimportant shit. Like where to allocate a few hundred dollars, which is chump change. Many of the people seemed as though they were cut throat, trying to one up one another. They squabbled over little stuff. I think they need to get their shit straight before they waste every body's time.

62

Well, what to do? I'm laid up at the start of my spring break with either a severe sprain or a broken ankle. This isn't good because I'm planning on going to the beach in two days. I hope it's only sprained. Anyway, before I find out if it's sprained, I want to talk about the future, or the near future shall I say. Going to the beach should be a good time. I only know two of the eight people, so it should be interesting. Spencer also said there's a good looking girl going by herself which I can't complain about.

I did want to talk about a certain girl though. I mentioned her before, Rachel. I don't know man. We had a conversation last week at work. She seems like a nice girl, the kind you take home to mom. We get along pretty well. I also feel something between us. I know I said she was cute last time, but on a good day she could be classified as hot. Anyway, while we were talking I found out that she doesn't have a boyfriend, but apparently she has a lot of friends who are guys. We know who else was like that. Well, I'm actually contemplating whether I should pursue her. The attraction is there, but she told me she's religious. Me, three months ago, would ultimately dismiss Rachel for her religious zeal, that of Christianity. I guess this is my first challenge or test. From what I've learned from the past the best thing I can do is go after this girl, if I'm interested, which so far I am. So it's settled. I'll do it right this time as I have learned from past mistakes.

63

I told the psychologist today that I thought there were two different stages in my life. When I went to live with my Dad in my sophomore year I reached a low point. My grades dropped off, I didn't care, and I hated it. For my junior year it was alright. By my senior year though, it was really bad; maybe my lowest point ever. Then, when I went to college, it got better. I felt independent and free for the first time in awhile. Then by the middle of the summer, after I broke up with Maggie, everything went sour again. I feel like I'm just going through the motions. There were few times in the past half year I felt alive. I don't know what I'm doing. I mean, I have a plan for school and such, but it's like I'm just going through it. It feels like I'm in limbo. This feeling of "depression" is different than the first time. It's like after I broke up I had a loss of innocence. I used to be so optimistic and the world was good and I felt like a king, like it was all coming together for me. In an instant, I lost that. It's like now I don't even want to meet people. I want that back. I want to learn, to explore, and to live. I want that youthful optimism back, my sense of humor back, my innocence

April 9, 2002

64

I felt optimistic today. So far, today has been a good day and I've felt good. While I'm still waiting on Chapel Hill's decision, I'm biding my time down here. Today felt really good though because I got back into it with this girl who sits next to me in Sociology of Marriage and Family. I may have mentioned her before, but today I just let go with her. For the entire class I just let go. I didn't pay attention and I just talked to her. At the end of the class we didn't realize we had a writing assignment, like everything passed us by. It felt really good. It was like the first time in awhile that I've been interested in someone. By this I mean, she's the first person I've cared to know about in a long time. This may sound weird, but I actually wanted to know about her. I also flirted with her, which is good because I honestly haven't even flirted with someone in a long time. Sure, I may be interested in her, and flirt with her because she's beautiful, but at least I'm doing it. Apparently she has a boyfriend for like five years and she's only twenty-one. That's a long time to be going out with somebody. It sounds like a change would be in good order. She also said her boyfriend took her to a strip club three weekends in a row. Sounds like an asshole to me. We'll see.

April 11, 2002

65

I like the new song by Jack Johnson. Anyway, there's a lot I want to talk about, so I may as well get started. Quickly, I must say that girl whose boyfriend is seemingly an asshole, apparently is content with her man. I sensed no discontent, so that mission is aborted. But I would like to give my psychological analysis of her anyway. She said she was Catholic and went to Catholic school, but she wasn't religious. She also smokes, had sex when she was fifteen and has been going out with the same guy for five years. I don't think she is in control of her life. She just goes along with things, aka, she's a follower. She's a simple person she doesn't care about much of anything very much. She has her own experiences and is unique in this way. Well, Spencer just called and invited me down the beach this weekend, but I'd have to blow off work. I don't know, I really need the money. Anyway, speaking of work, I will segue into my next prospect, certainly the most serious of them all.

Azar made me a bet. He said he would pay me one hundred dollars if I bring a girl back to my room and we have sex. The money would be good and I can use some good old tension relieving sex before finals. So, I will win the bet, and get my money and my sex. So let me cover my latest prospect. I came into work today training as a waiter. She was already there as a waitress, and she immediately stole my attention. She is about five foot, six inches tall and has brown hair. She pulled it back into a pippy long stocking and it looked cute. Her body was okay, as much as one can tell from the work uniform, but she had a pretty face. We had to watch the alcoholic videos together because she is training too. So we got to talking. Turns out… I'll get back to you on it.

April 13, 2002

66

I really should be going to bed, but I just wanted to say that I deleted all of my old emails. Hopefully now I can move on. I also wanted to say that although I'm over it, I still want to see Maggie when I go home this summer. Even if it's just a few times, reading our old emails it reminds me of how good she made me feel those couple of years when I was stuck at my Dad's house. I realize that we went through some shit, but I think it's still worth it. Also about those emails, I saw something. I saw what I lost from a year ago, since we broke up. I lost that carelessness, that youthful optimism, that playful attitude. I saw it in my emails with both Jen and Maggie. For more than a year I was making good progress socially, girls specifically. After the break up I can see how much I regressed. Hopefully though, I can get back to where I was with the knowledge from my experience.

April 16, 2002

67

Sometimes it feels like no matter what you do, or how hard you try, a little thing called fate keeps bringing you back down to reality. It's like when you're so close to something you want so badly, and fate says, "Fuck you, you mean you actually thought you had a chance?" So, I guess it was a pipe dream. I did not get into Carolina. For two years, I made it my goal to make it in. I did everything I'm capable of and I gave it everything, put myself out on a line, and took my best shot. It didn't matter. I was never going to go to Chapel Hill. My life would have been too easy then. I literally made it my mission the past two years to get in. I gave up on a social life and I cut myself off from the world and made this my sole focus. I swear it's just like the Rudy movie. I wanted to get in so much to prove to everyone one that has ever knocked me, all my teachers, friends, parents, and to me that I was capable of greatness. I deserved to get in more than any other person at that school. I earned it. All those hours studying, all those one hundred percents on exams, they don't mean shit. I think this is a great turning point in my life. I am now destined to walk amongst the masses of ignorant common folk. I don't belong.

April 24, 2002

68

I guess I haven't written since I was denied entry to Chapel Hill. I think I'll get over it. The thing is, that not getting in was such a shock. There wasn't a doubt in my mind that I would get in and when I didn't, I was amazed. My whole plan, and everything I had worked for was thrown out the window. I guess I have to start over. Make a new plan.

So here it is. I'm going to apply to Penn State and Pitt. I already got into Maryland. So we'll see. Now, to address the next three weeks at UNC – Charlotte, the last three weeks of me being there. I guess now's not the time to make those personal connections. I'm heading back north, but I have a couple of things I can do. I can get a four point zero for the first time in my life. I can also try to have a threesome with Jen from work. This would make for a memorable time at school. Go out with a bang as they say. Once I move north I get to make new connections and make some new friends/girlfriends. Oh, by the way, I'm on a plane now back down to Charlotte.

69

Its eleven thirty on a Monday night and I have approximately two weeks left in North Carolina before I return home for the summer and maybe the rest of my life. I want to get a four point zero GPA. Then I will prove to my parents, my friends, everybody, that although I didn't get into Carolina, I stuck it out and I'm doing something of greatness. I'm nervous, but I think if I put the work in for the next two weeks I can do it.

In schools news, I should hear from Virginia this week, but it's a likely negative response. I don't see how's it's possible. A little feeling inside me thinks there's a chance, but I expect the worst in this instance. This summer should be better. This is the summer to try to fix all of the problems at home. I now must face what I've been hiding from for two years. Now that I have a better understanding of myself I can work with everyone at home. I am an essentialist. I think all problems can be broken down into an essential feature. I should ask somebody, maybe Jen, to the Center City Fest. It should be good.

70

Its four minutes after twelve on a Sunday night and I probably should be studying for my finals. I would be, but some things have been distracting me; nothing major, but enough to distract me. This whole thing with Carolina has been distracting and has taken some motivation from me. I just talked to Neeb and he said he might be going to Penn State next year, so that would be cool to have someone to live with. He said he got in on a three point four-five GPA, so I should get in. Anyway, I guess that's good.

I went to the Center City Fest with some people from work. It's like I'm just starting to make friends and now I have to leave and to indulge further. At the concert there was this girl, Melissa, from work. She is average looking, I guess in work clothes, but I really didn't know her very well. At the concert we got to talking and it turns out we have a lot in common. She is also from PA, and we go to school together. The thing is that we had a great connection. Being that we were at a crowded concert, people were pushing and shit, so I stood behind her, and fended them off. And like from a scene in a movie, a couple of times she got knocked back into my arms. And at about that time, I started to kick myself. I mean, I've been down here for two years, worked at this restaurant for half a year, and don't talk to this girl. Two weeks before I go home for good, I meet this great person who I can really relate to. I mean, why didn't I open myself up sooner? All this time, and it was right there in front of me. When I go to my new school next year, I can't waste time. I have to open up to the people so that I may experience life. I must get a four point zero GPA.

71

I'm the king of the castle and you're the dirty rascal, crash into me. Well, in the most unlikely turn of events, I was put on Virginia's waiting list. I was almost convinced that I would get denied, but it's like as soon as I accept my average place in college, going to Pitt, I am thrown for a loop yet again. I don't quite know what to say. I've been on an emotional rollercoaster. This rollercoaster just took an upward turn, but why should I really get excited? I mean, right now it's a numbers game. I'll probably do well again academically, so it's off of me, and on them. It's out of my hands. If enough folks decide not to attend, I might get in, but not necessarily. I'm sure it will be another month before I find out whether I've been admitted or not. I can't pump myself up for this like I did for Carolina. It will just get me hurt. All of this said, I am still proud of myself that I made it this far. In two quick years I went from barely being accepted to college, to being on the verge of being accepted to one of the world's best schools. This is unthinkable. While it sounds self centered to say, I feel like saying, "Get on my shoulders, I will carry you to the promise land." Of course I can't, but I feel like saying it.

72

I'm studying for my American history test. If I've, wait, this is the worst kind of history. I love European history, war history, and Asian history. I love to learn about a lot of history, but I do not find US history at all appealing. While kings were being executed in Europe, a bunch of back woods rich boys were looking for a way to get the most power possible in a backwater hole of an unimportant place called America.

If I've learned one thing from US history, it's that it's a mess. No one comes out clean. In grade school they sugar coat it, make it all pretty, in reality, they were all scumbags. While trying to "uphold the constitution," plenty of people went above their democratic power to manipulate the system to their liking. I don't like it. All they preach about freedom, and all the rest, they're full of shit. If I step out of line they're going to slam me.

May 25, 2002

73

It's a sad situation and I'm listening to Marshal Crenshaw. I'm home on summer break and in the midst of everything I want to talk about the reoccurring Maggie, because I saw her car and her dad when I drove by. I just want to tell her how I feel and what I think about the past and what not. I will then be done with it, but I want to say my piece and be done. I think she's a cool chick and I'd like to continue it, but things have been fucked up. This song is reminiscing of times missed. I know I built it up, but I think I need to relive the experience and to revisit the ghosts to get rid of all the shit and start anew. She's a good person, and it was my bad.

74

It seems the closer I get to finish this journal, the harder it is to write in it. Anyway, while I revealed my plan to be a revolutionary leader to my father, there is a matter of slightly less importance. I am in the first moderately serious relationship following Maggie. It's this girl, Stacy. She fits the bill of what I was looking for. She is nothing spectacular, but there is potential. She's nothing to write home about but she likes me a lot. For whatever reason, I'm not very emotionally attached or desperate. It's like whatever happens is cool with me. If she wants to go out, or she never calls me again, it's all the same to me. So far she's pretty cool about everything. To something else, I think I have gotten much better at identifying "my type."

75

Finally, I have a free minute. It's like the last couple of days have been strange. I went down the beach with Jay from work. The plan was to get a hotel room for the night and come home on Saturday afternoon. These plans changed however, when at three fifteen in the morning we were evicted from the hotel. Apparently, Jay had been throwing nitrous cartridges over the balcony at people. Luckily, we didn't get cited, but like I said, we were evicted and there were a lot of pigs in our room. Matt had come with me and he was really anger, running his mouth about every which thing. I wasn't angry; I knew what Jay was like before I went down. I actually liked it. I wasn't really scared when the police came in.

July 23, 2002

76

I just saw *Bridget Jones Diary*, and it got me thinking. My life is going to change in a month, but it doesn't really feel like it right now. I'm starting to settle down into the summer and things don't feel like they're going to change.